D0536995

THE BEST OF
SPAIN

THE BEST OF
SPAIN
A COOKBOOK

Evie Righter, Series Editor

Recipes and text by Alicia Saacs
Food Photography by Steven Mark Need

CollinsPublishersSanFrancisco
A Division of HarperCollins*Publishers*

First published in USA 1993 by Collins Publishers San Francisco
1160 Battery Street, San Francisco, CA 94111

Produced by Smallwood and Stewart Inc.,
New York City

© 1993 Smallwood and Stewart, Inc.

Edited by Alice Wong
Jacket design by Carol Bokuniewicz
Food styling by Sandra Robishaw
Prop styling by Bette Blau

Photography credits: John Blake/Picture Perfect: 17. Jean S.
Buldain/Picture Perfect: 1; 43. Mike Busselle/Picture Perfect: 7; 27; 32. Bill
Holden/Picture Perfect: 69. Michael J. Howell/Picture Perfect: 2-3.
Kiernan/Picture Perfect: 85. Picture Perfect: 91.

Library of Congress Cataloging-in-Publication Data

Righter, Evie.
    The best of Spain : a cookbook / Evie Righter : recipes by Alicia
Saacs : food photography by Steven Mark Needham
        p.   cm.
    Includes index.
    ISBN 0-00-255207-8 : $14.95
    1. Cookery, Spanish. 2. Cookery–Spain. I. Title.
    641.5946–dc20

Printed in Hong Kong

Contents

Introduction

The cooking of Spain may well be the least known and most misunderstood of the world's great cuisines. All too often, Spanish cooking is equated with Mexican cooking, which is quite erroneous because it is not at all hot and spicy. In fact, it is a cuisine unto itself, which relies on the robust Mediterranean flavors of garlic, olive oil, peppers, and tomatoes, and blends them with the more unusual tastes contributed by the Moors, who ruled Spain for nearly eight hundred years.

The Spanish way of preparing foods is really much closer in style to French and Italian than to anything from the New World. Of course, Europe has Spain to thank for introducing native American foods ‒ peppers, tomatoes, potatoes, corn, and chocolate ‒ to the Old World, and one wonders how European cooking existed for so long without them.

Spanish cuisine was shaped both by Spain's remarkable history and by its unusual geography and climate that compress the variety of a whole continent into one relatively small country. Moorish rule imparted Eastern accents to Spanish food, still evident today in the use of saffron, cumin, coriander, almonds, and rice. Geographically, an extensive coastline makes seafood an important feature of the Spanish

A goatherd in the town of Mérida, Extremadura

diet and the inspiration for some of the country's most characteristic dishes, like *merluza a la vasca* (hake in green sauce). The rugged mountains of the interior generally do not support cattle, so game, lamb, and pork (as well as pork products, like cured ham and chorizo sausage) are more typical than beef. Sheep's milk cheese is more common than cheese made from cow's milk. Dried legumes, adaptable to a variety of climates and terrains, are the basis for such popular dishes as *cocido madrileño* (boiled beef and vegetables Madrid style).

From the craggy green north to the fertile lands of La Rioja along the upper Ebro River, which produce celebrated wines, to the arid central tablelands - the breadbasket of Spain - to the hot south, where olive trees thrive and sherry wines are made, Spain is a mosaic of mini-countries, and this accounts for the very regional nature of Spanish cooking. Except for a few shared ingredients, it is not possible to speak of a national cuisine. But simplicity is a common characteristic and the key to Spanish cooking, which uses the finest and freshest ingredients in preparations that allow the natural flavors to shine through. Sauces do not compete with foods but act as subtle complements to them, especially in the case of seafood. *Gambas al ajillo* (garlic shrimp), *pescado a la sal* (fish baked in salt), and *vieiras a la gallega* (scallops baked with cured ham) clearly follow that philosophy. And desserts -

never a particularly important part of a Spanish meal ~ tend to be comforting creations based on eggs, milk, cinnamon, and lemon.

Clearly, Spanish cooking is by no means exotic, but it excels at using down-to-earth ingredients in uncommon ways. The potato and onion omelet, *tortilla española*; the cold soup, *gazpacho*; and the world-renowned *paella* are delicious examples of Spanish cooks' flair for creating excitement with everyday foods.

In a category apart are Spain's *tapas* ~ appetizer foods that are offered before lunch and again before dinner in thousands of bars across the country. They come in endless varieties. Just about anything in a small portion can become a *tapa*, and *tapas* provide the opportunity to "graze" in a casual and spirited atmosphere filled with culinary pleasures.

The recipes presented in *The Best of Spain* give a sampling of some of the most traditional dishes from Spain's many regional cuisines. Of course, elegant restaurants in Spain today serve *nouvelle*-style cooking and experiment with nontraditional ingredients. But for the visitor to Spain, or for the cook interested in re-creating the incredibly appealing and inviting flavors of the country, the time-honored dishes that have survived the centuries are those that prove to be the most tantalizing and the most gratifying.

Aceitunas Aliñadas & Pincho Moruno, page 16

Aceitunas Aliñadas

Marinated Green Olives

More olive trees grow in Andalusia in southern Spain than anywhere else in the world. Olives are a typical appetizer and go particularly well with a glass of chilled dry sherry, which also comes from Andalusia. The longer these olives marinate, the better they become.

1-pound jar large Spanish green olives with pits, drained & well rinsed

2 lemon wedges

2 tablespoons fruity extra-virgin olive oil

½ cup red wine vinegar

6 garlic cloves, lightly crushed & peeled

2 or 3 sprigs fresh thyme or 1 teaspoon dried

2 bay leaves

1 teaspoon dried oregano

½ teaspoon paprika

⅛ teaspoon freshly ground pepper

1 teaspoon cumin seeds, crushed, or ground cumin

1 teaspoon fennel seeds

With a sharp knife, make a small slit in each olive to allow the marinade to penetrate. Place the olives in a glass jar. Add the remaining ingredients and enough water to completely cover the olives. Cover the jar. Shake well, refrigerate, and allow to marinate for at least a few days, preferably for more than 2 weeks. The olives will keep in the refrigerator for many months. Makes about 3 cups.

Tortilla Española

POTATO AND ONION OMELET

Served all over Spain, *tortilla* is a well-loved and versatile dish
that can be eaten at breakfast, later in the day as a *tapa*,
or as a light supper. It may well become one of
your family's favorites.

Olive oil

2½ pounds baking potatoes,
peeled & sliced ⅛ inch
thick

Salt

½ medium onion, thinly sliced

4 large eggs

Preheat the oven to 350°F. Grease a 13-by-9-inch roasting pan with 2 teaspoons oil. Arrange a layer of potatoes in the pan, sprinkle with salt, and scatter with some of the onion. Drizzle with oil. Continue to make layers with remaining potatoes and onion, using 3 tablespoons oil in all. Roast for 45 minutes, loosening and turning potatoes occasionally with a metal spatula.

In a large bowl, using a fork, beat the eggs until uniform in color. Season with salt. Add the potatoes and onion, separating them as much as possible and pressing down with the spatula so that they are covered with egg. Let sit about 10 minutes.

Heat 1 tablespoon oil in an 8- or 9-inch skillet. Quickly add the egg-potato mixture, flatten with the spatula, and reduce heat to medium-high. Shake skillet constantly to prevent sticking. When the underside begins to brown, slide the omelet onto a plate. Place another plate

over it, and flip. Heat 1 teaspoon oil in the skillet, remove the top plate from the omelet, and slide it back into the skillet, smoothing out any rough edges with the spatula and continuing to shake the skillet. Brown lightly, turn again, and cook until egg is just set. Slice in wedges or small squares and serve hot or at room temperature. Serves 8 to 10 as a *tapa;* 4 as a main course.

Pa Amb Tomàquet

Catalan Country Bread *(picture p. 21)*

Commonly served as an accompaniment to a meal in
the region of Catalunya (Catalonia), this bread, rubbed
with garlic and tomato and drizzled with olive oil, is a
delicious departure from plain table bread. As a *tapa*, it is
often topped with a thin slice of cured ham or with anchovy
fillets. Because of its simplicity, the ingredients must be the
best: coarse-textured crusty bread, flavorful olive
oil, and vine-ripened tomatoes.

6 long bread slices, ½ inch
    thick, from a large round
    loaf

2 large garlic cloves, cut in
    half crosswise

2 ripe, juicy tomatoes, cut in
    half crosswise

Several tablespoons fruity
    extra-virgin olive oil

Coarse salt

Preheat the oven to 350°F. Arrange the bread slices on a baking sheet and toast lightly on both sides. Let cool.

Rub the cut side of a garlic clove over both sides of each bread slice. Then rub the bread on both sides with the cut sides of the tomatoes, squeezing each tomato half slightly to release its juice. Drizzle with the oil and sprinkle with salt. Serves 6 as a *tapa*.

Setas Salteadas

Sautéed Mushrooms with Parsley and Garlic

The taste of fresh mushrooms sautéed in olive oil and sprinkled with parsley and garlic is universally appealing. Either wild or cultivated mushrooms (or both) may be used for this *tapa*, which takes only minutes to make and should be served immediately.

1 pound wild or cultivated mushrooms, wiped clean

2 tablespoons olive oil

Salt & freshly ground pepper

2 tablespoons minced parsley

2 garlic cloves, minced

Lemon juice

If the mushrooms are very small, trim stems and leave whole; otherwise, cut them in half or quarter them. Heat the oil in a large skillet and sauté the mushrooms over high heat for 1 minute. Season with salt and pepper and sprinkle with the parsley and garlic. Continue cooking briefly until mushrooms have softened, about 2 to 3 minutes. Drizzle mushrooms with lemon juice and serve at once. Serves 6 to 8 as a *tapa*.

Pincho Moruno

Spiced Skewered Pork *(picture p. 10)*

The spices that season these mini-kabobs evoke the
centuries of Moorish influence on Spanish cooking. Ideally,
the meat should be grilled, but it can equally well be broiled.
You can also serve these kabobs as an entrée. Simply cut the
meat into 1½-inch cubes and cook for about 6 minutes.
They are particularly good accompanied by
Poor Man's Potatoes (p. 40).

1 garlic clove, minced

1 teaspoon ground cumin

¼ teaspoon ground coriander

1 teaspoon paprika

¼ teaspoon crushed red pepper

¼ teaspoon salt

Freshly ground pepper

2 tablespoons olive oil

1 pound boneless pork loin, cut
   in 1-inch cubes

In a medium bowl, combine all the ingredients except the pork. Add pork and stir to coat thoroughly with marinade. Cover and refrigerate several hours or overnight, stirring occasionally.

Remove pork from marinade and thread onto 4 short skewers. Grill over a hot charcoal fire or broil 4 inches from flame, turning once, until meat is just cooked but still juicy, about 4 minutes. Serves 4 as a *tapa*.

A village street in Málaga, Andalusia

Gambas al Ajillo

Garlic Shrimp

In Spain, this is a favorite *tapa,* served sizzling hot in shallow earthenware casseroles called *cazuelas.* Good crusty bread is a must for dunking in the sauce.

¾ pound small shrimp in their shells

Salt

4 tablespoons olive oil

4 garlic cloves, sliced

1 small dried red chili pepper, seeds removed & cut in half, or ¼ teaspoon crushed red pepper

1 tablespoon lemon juice

1 tablespoon dry white wine

2 tablespoons minced parsley

Shell the shrimp. (It is not necessary to devein them.) Sprinkle with salt.

Heat the oil, garlic, and chili pepper in a shallow flameproof casserole over medium-high heat. When the garlic is just beginning to brown, add the shrimp and cook, stirring, about 1 minute, or until just done and firm to the touch. Stir in the lemon juice, wine, and parsley. Serve immediately, preferably in the casserole. Serves 4 to 6 as a *tapa.*

Almejas a la Marinera

Clams with Garlic and White Wine

The clams used for this tasty dish, which is found in most
tapas bars in Spain, should be as small as possible. Use
littleneck clams or cockles, and serve good bread to mop up
the garlicky green sauce.

2 dozen small clams,
  thoroughly scrubbed

1 tablespoon cornmeal or flour

3 tablespoons olive oil

4 tablespoons minced onion

3 garlic cloves, minced

½ cup dry white wine

¼ cup Fish Stock (p. 62)

1 tablespoon lemon juice

1 bay leaf

3 tablespoons minced parsley

Freshly ground pepper

Put the clams in a bowl, cover them with salted cold water, and sprinkle with cornmeal. Refrigerate, uncovered, several hours or overnight to rid clams of sand.

Drain, rinse, and dry clams. Heat the oil in a large, shallow flameproof casserole and sauté the onion and garlic over high heat. Just before the garlic begins to brown, add clams and cook, stirring, about 3 minutes. Add the wine and let it cook off. Stir in the stock, lemon juice, bay leaf, 1 tablespoon parsley, and pepper. Reduce heat to medium, cover, and cook, removing clams as they open to a warm platter; add a little water if the liquid evaporates before all the clams have opened. (The finished dish should have some sauce.) Return the opened clams to the casserole, heat 1 minute, and sprinkle with remaining parsley. Serves 6 to 8 as a *tapa*.

Almejas a la Marinera & Pa Amb Tomàquet, page 14

21

Mejillones en Vinagreta

Mussels Vinaigrette

Mussels marinated in this manner and presented on the half shell are colorful party fare that is always sure to please. Buy mussels that are tightly closed; they are the freshest.

2 dozen mussels, scrubbed & debearded

1 tablespoon cornmeal or flour

9 tablespoons olive oil

3 tablespoons lemon juice

2 tablespoons minced Spanish onion

2 tablespoons finely chopped pimiento (p. 36)

3 tablespoons minced parsley

Salt & freshly ground pepper

1 hard-boiled egg, minced

Put the mussels in a bowl, cover them with salted cold water, and sprinkle with cornmeal. Refrigerate, uncovered, several hours or overnight to rid mussels of sand.

Drain and rinse mussels. In a covered skillet, steam mussels with ½ cup water over high heat. Remove mussels as they open and discard any that do not open. Separate mussels from their shells and reserve half of each shell. Clean shells well and refrigerate.

In a large bowl, whisk together oil and lemon juice. Stir in the onion, pimiento, 2 tablespoons parsley, and salt and pepper. Add mussels and stir. Cover and refrigerate several hours or overnight.

To serve, return mussels to chilled half shells, spoon some marinade over them, and sprinkle with egg and remaining parsley. Arrange on a serving platter. Serves 4 to 6 as a *tapa*.

Salpicón de Mariscos

Marinated Shellfish

Serve this refreshing mix of shellfish as a *tapa* or arrange on a bed of lettuce as a first course. You can vary the shellfish according to what is available. Small mussels, with or without shells, and chunk crabmeat are possible additions or substitutions.

One 1½-pound live lobster or 2 frozen lobster tails

¾ pound medium-large shrimp in their shells

¼ pound bay scallops, or sea scallops cut in halves

10 tablespoons olive oil

3 tablespoons sherry wine vinegar

1 tablespoon capers, chopped

3 small scallions, finely chopped

1 garlic clove, minced

1 small ripe tomato, chopped

½ green bell pepper, finely chopped

1 tablespoon minced parsley

Salt & freshly ground pepper

Bring 12 cups salted water to a boil over high heat, add the lobster, cover, and cook about 15 minutes. Remove lobster to a platter and let cool. Pour off half the water, bring the remaining water to a boil, and add the shrimp and scallops. Cook about 1 minute, or until just done. Remove shrimp and scallops to a plate and let cool. Shell lobster and shrimp; cut lobster into chunks.

In a large bowl, whisk together the oil and vinegar. Stir in the remaining ingredients and gently mix in the shellfish. Cover and refrigerate several hours or overnight. Serves 6 as a *tapa*.

Sopa de Ajo

Garlic Soup

A traditional peasant dish, this soup in its simplest rendition relies upon the most basic of ingredients: water, garlic, and bread. It will, of course, admit embellishments that provide greater depth of flavor, such as using broth instead of water and adding ham and paprika. It is also quite common to poach eggs in the finished broth.

7 cups chicken broth

2 beef bones

1 head garlic, separated into cloves, unpeeled, plus 8 cloves, peeled & chopped

4 parsley sprigs

Salt & freshly ground pepper

2½ to 3 tablespoons olive oil

¼ pound cured ham, such as prosciutto, sliced ¼ inch thick & diced

1 tablespoon paprika

½ teaspoon ground cumin

8 bread slices, ¼ inch thick, from a long narrow loaf

4 large eggs, if desired

In a large saucepan, combine the broth, bones, garlic head, parsley, and salt and pepper. Bring to a boil, reduce heat to medium, and simmer, uncovered, for 30 minutes. Strain into another saucepan. (You should have about 6 cups soup.)

Meanwhile, heat 1 tablespoon oil in a medium skillet and sauté the chopped garlic over medium heat until lightly golden. Add the ham and cook 1 minute. Stir in the paprika and cumin and remove immediately from heat. Add the garlic mixture to the soup and simmer.

Preheat the oven to 350°F. Arrange

Olive groves near Jaén, Andalusia

bread slices on a baking sheet and brush lightly on both sides with oil. Bake, turning once, until golden on both sides, about 5 minutes.

Place the toasted bread in a soup tureen and pour in the hot soup. (If adding eggs, use a heatproof tureen, slide them into the soup, and bake at 450°F. until set, about 3 to 4 minutes.) Serves 4.

Caldo Gallego

Hearty Galician Soup

In Galicia, in the northwestern corner of Spain, *grelos*, a vegetable similar to Swiss chard, grows everywhere; it is an important ingredient in this soup. Known the world over, *caldo gallego* also includes beans, meats, and potatoes; it can easily serve as a complete meal.

¼ pound dried white beans, such as Great Northern

10 cups water

2 beef or ham bones

1 leek, well washed

½ pound beef chuck, very lean & meaty pork short ribs, or fresh ham hocks

¼ pound salt pork or slab bacon, cut in 1-inch cubes

2 medium red potatoes, peeled & quartered

1½ cups chopped Swiss chard, collard greens, or kale, thick stems trimmed

Salt & freshly ground pepper

Cover beans with cold water and soak overnight. Drain and rinse.

In a large soup pot, combine beans with the water, bones, leek, beef, and salt pork. Bring to a boil, cover, and simmer for 1½ to 2 hours, or until beans are almost done. Add the potatoes, Swiss chard, and salt and pepper and cook 30 minutes. Turn off the heat, cover, and let sit 15 minutes or more to thicken.

Remove the leek and the beef, if using, cut into pieces, return to soup, and reheat. Serves 4 to 6.

Gazpacho a la Andaluza

R e d   G a z p a c h o

There are few things more refreshing on a hot summer's day than a chilled bowl of gazpacho. Often called a liquid salad, gazpacho is very low in calories but filled with nutrients. If they are available, use vine-ripened tomatoes; if not, a combination of fresh tomatoes and canned gives good results.

1 pound fresh tomatoes, cut in pieces

1 pound canned plum tomatoes, with juices

1 green bell pepper, cut in pieces

2 teaspoons sugar

¼ teaspoon ground cumin

4 tablespoons sherry wine vinegar or 5 tablespoons red wine vinegar

2 tablespoons olive oil

1 cup cold water

2 Kirby cucumbers or 1 small cucumber, peeled & cut in pieces

½ small onion, halved

2 garlic cloves, chopped

Salt

Small croutons & finely chopped tomato, cucumber, & green bell pepper for garnish, if desired

Combine all the ingredients except garnish in a food processor in batches and blend until pureed. Strain into a bowl, pressing with the back of a spoon to extract all the liquid. Adjust vinegar and salt to taste.

Cover and refrigerate several hours or overnight. (The gazpacho gains in flavor if chilled overnight.) Garnish the soup as desired just before serving. Serves 6.

Gazpacho a la Andaluza & Ajo Blanco de Málaga, page 33

Ajo Blanco de Málaga

Málaga White Gazpacho with Grapes
(picture p. 31)

Gazpacho need not be red ~ indeed, long before the arrival of the tomato from the New World, gazpachos such as this were a diet staple in southern Spain. Ground almonds give this soup the pristine whiteness that its name suggests and the grapes add an interesting contrast of taste and texture.

3 large slices good-quality
    white bread, crusts
    removed

3 garlic cloves

1 teaspoon salt

¼ pound blanched almonds

½ cup olive oil

3 to 5 tablespoons red wine
    vinegar

4 cups ice water

3 dozen seedless green grapes,
    peeled, or 1 cup chopped
    peeled apple for garnish

Soak the bread in water until softened, then squeeze out most of the water. Combine bread, garlic, salt, and almonds in a food processor and blend to a paste. With the motor running, add the oil in a thin stream, then gradually add the vinegar and ice water. Strain into a bowl, pressing with the back of a spoon to extract all the liquid. Adjust vinegar and salt to taste. Cover and refrigerate several hours or overnight. (The gazpacho gains in flavor if chilled overnight.) Garnish with the grapes just before serving. Serves 6.

Waterfront in San Sebastián

Pisto Manchego

Manchegan Vegetable Medley

The region of La Mancha ~ Don Quixote's country ~ is not known for exceptional gastronomy. Nevertheless, Manchegan sheep's milk cheese and this medley of zucchini, tomatoes, and peppers are famous throughout Spain. You may cook this dish until the vegetables are quite soft, or leave them slightly crisp. The stew can be served hot or at room temperature ~ in which case you may want to add a touch of olive oil and lemon juice. With the addition of boiled potatoes, this becomes a healthy one-course meal.

2 tablespoons olive oil

2 onions, chopped

3 garlic cloves, minced

2 tablespoons diced cured ham, such as prosciutto

2 green bell peppers, cut in 1-inch pieces

1½ pounds ripe tomatoes, peeled & cubed

2 medium zucchini, cubed

1 tablespoon minced parsley

½ teaspoon dried oregano

2 tablespoons dry white wine

Salt & freshly ground pepper

Heat the oil in a deep pot and sauté the onions, garlic, ham, and green peppers over medium-high heat until the onion is wilted. Stir in the tomatoes and cook 5 minutes. Add the zucchini, parsley, oregano, and wine, and season with salt and pepper. Simmer, covered, 15 minutes. Uncover and cook off some of the liquid over high heat, if necessary. Serves 4 to 6.

Escalivada

This dish is simplicity itself and makes an excellent first course or accompaniment to roasted or grilled meat, especially pork. A drizzle of extra-virgin olive oil before serving adds to its robust Mediterranean flavor. You can roast the vegetables in the oven or grill them over hot coals. Follow this preparation of red bell peppers to make the pimientos called for in many Spanish recipes. Pimientos may be kept covered in the refrigerator for several days.

2 small eggplants

2 green bell peppers

2 red bell peppers

2 medium onions, peeled

Extra-virgin olive oil

Coarse salt

1 tablespoon minced parsley

Preheat the oven to 500°F. Grease a 13-by-9-inch roasting pan and in it arrange the eggplants, green and red peppers, and onions. Brush with oil and roast, turning once, for 20 minutes. Remove from oven and let cool.

Skin the eggplants and peppers. Remove some of the seeds from the eggplants and cut into lengthwise strips. Seed the peppers and cut into strips. Cut the onions into slivers.

Arrange the vegetables on a platter or on individual plates. Drizzle with oil, then sprinkle with salt and parsley. Serves 4 to 6.

Acelgas con Pasas y Piñones

Sautéed Greens with Raisins and Pine Nuts

Greens ~ similar to Swiss chard or collard greens ~ are a favored vegetable in Spain and are particularly well liked in combination with two other Spanish products, raisins and pine nuts.

¼ cup dark raisins

1¼ pounds Swiss chard or other leafy greens, such as spinach, escarole, or collard greens, thick stems trimmed

2 tablespoons olive oil

2 large garlic cloves, lightly crushed

3 tablespoons minced onion

3 tablespoons pine nuts

Salt & freshly ground pepper

In a small bowl, cover the raisins with hot water and let stand 10 minutes. Drain.

Chop the Swiss chard coarsely. Heat the oil in a large skillet and sauté the garlic and onion over medium-high heat until onion is wilted. Add the greens, turn heat to high, and stir-fry 1 or 2 minutes.

Drain raisins and add them with pine nuts to skillet. Season with salt and pepper. Combine well, cover, and cook slowly over low heat for a few minutes until the greens are as soft as desired. Serves 4.

Habas a la Catalana

Lima Beans Catalan Style

If you can find fresh fava beans, which are what Spanish cooks use for this recipe, by all means use them. The dish is served at room temperature and can act as either a vegetable or salad course. "Catalan style," in this instance, refers to the fresh mint that lends its distinctive perfume to the beans.

1 pound fresh or frozen lima beans or fresh fava beans

Salt & freshly ground pepper

1 small scallion

2 sprigs fresh mint plus 2 teaspoons chopped fresh mint

1 bay leaf

½ teaspoon Dijon-style mustard

1 tablespoon sherry wine vinegar

2 tablespoons olive oil

1 garlic clove, minced

1 tablespoon minced parsley

2 teaspoons chopped fresh thyme or ¼ teaspoon dried

2 ounces cured ham, such as prosciutto, cut in julienne strips

½ head Boston lettuce, shredded

Place the beans in a saucepan and cover them with the water. Add the salt and pepper, scallion, mint sprigs, and bay leaf. Bring to a boil and simmer, covered, about 30 minutes, or until the beans are tender.

In a large serving bowl, whisk together the mustard and vinegar. Whisk in the oil, garlic, chopped mint, parsley, thyme, and salt and pepper.

Drain the beans, remove the bay leaf, and add the beans to the vinaigrette with the ham and lettuce. Toss to combine and garnish with more mint sprigs. Serves 4.

Patatas Pobres

P o o r   M a n ' s   P o t a t o e s

Despite their name, these potatoes, which are simply sliced,
sautéed, and sprinkled with garlic and parsley, are perfectly at
home with the most elegant dishes.

3 tablespoons olive oil

*4 medium baking potatoes,
peeled & sliced ⅛ inch
thick*

Salt

1 tablespoon minced garlic

1 tablespoon minced parsley

Heat the oil in a large skillet over high heat. Reduce heat to medium-high, arrange a single layer of potatoes in the pan, and sprinkle with salt. Turn with a metal spatula to coat the potatoes with the oil. Add another layer of potatoes and salt, and turn to coat. Repeat with the remaining potatoes. Cover and cook over medium heat, turning once, until potatoes are tender, about 20 minutes. Sprinkle with the garlic and parsley. Serves 4.

Patatas Pobres & Chuletas Aliñadas con Alioli, page 76

41

Patatas Bravas

Crisp Potatoes with Spicy Tomato Sauce

Although in Spain this dish is most frequently made with fried potatoes, the results are as good if not better when the potatoes are roasted. The spicy tomato sauce is added just before serving so that the potatoes stay crisp, and it should not completely cover them. *Patatas bravas* can also be served as a *tapa*.

1 tablespoon olive oil

1 bay leaf

1 garlic clove, lightly crushed

4 medium baking potatoes, peeled & cut as for large French fries

Salt & freshly ground pepper

Spicy Tomato Sauce:

1 tablespoon olive oil

2 tablespoons minced onion

1 garlic clove, minced

1 teaspoon sweet paprika

1 cup tomato sauce

Pinch of sugar

¼ teaspoon crushed red pepper or to taste

¼ cup dry white wine

1 teaspoon fresh thyme or ¼ teaspoon dried

1 tablespoon minced parsley

Salt & freshly ground pepper

Preheat the oven to 400°F. Grease a 13-by-9-inch roasting pan with the oil. Add the bay leaf, garlic, potatoes, and salt and pepper. Turn to coat potatoes with oil. Roast about 45 minutes, turning occasionally to keep the potatoes from sticking. The potatoes should be crusty and golden.

Meanwhile, make the Spicy Tomato

Burros for hire in Mijas, Málaga

Sauce. Heat the oil in a small saucepan and sauté the onion and garlic over medium-high heat until onion is wilted. Stir in the paprika, then add the remaining sauce ingredients. Bring to a boil and simmer, uncovered, 20 minutes. To serve, spoon some sauce over each portion of hot potatoes. Serves 4.

Ensalada Ilustrada con Vinagreta de Anchoa

Tuna, Asparagus, and Olive Salad with Anchovy Vinaigrette

Vine-ripened tomatoes, lettuce, and wonderfully sweet onions make up the standard Spanish salad. But with a few additions, such as those in this recipe, it becomes "illustrious."

About 4 cups romaine lettuce, torn in pieces

2 tomatoes, cut in chunks

½ small Spanish onion, thinly sliced

One 5-ounce can light meat tuna, packed in olive oil, drained

8 canned or bottled white asparagus spears

16 green olives, plain or stuffed with pimiento or anchovy

2 hard-boiled eggs, cut in quarters

Anchovy Vinaigrette:

6 tablespoons extra-virgin olive oil

2 tablespoons sherry wine vinegar

2 anchovy fillets, minced

1 small garlic clove, minced

1 tablespoon minced parsley

Salt & freshly ground pepper

Heap the lettuce on a serving platter and arrange the tomatoes and onion on top. Scatter chunks of tuna over the salad. Top with the asparagus, olives, and eggs.

To make the Anchovy Vinaigrette, in a small bowl, whisk together all its ingredients. Pour the vinaigrette over the salad. Serves 4 to 6.

Esqueixada

Dried Cod Salad with Olives, Tomato, and Bell Pepper

The salt cod in this Catalan salad is mild in flavor and firm in texture. You may not even recognize it as fish! With its rich black olives, sweet tomato, and crisp bell pepper, *esqueixada* is colorful and thoroughly refreshing. You can buy salt cod in many Italian delicatessens or at your fish market.

1 pound dried salt cod, skinned & deboned

1 small onion, slivered

24 cured black olives

1 medium tomato, cubed

1 red bell pepper, cut in thin rings

2 tablespoons minced parsley

½ cup extra-virgin olive oil

3 tablespoons red wine vinegar

2 garlic cloves, mashed through a garlic press

Salt

¼ teaspoon freshly ground pepper

Soak the cod in cold water to cover for 36 hours, changing the water occasionally. Drain cod and shred it with your fingers.

In a bowl, combine cod with the onion, olives, tomato, red pepper, and parsley.

In a small bowl, whisk together the oil, vinegar, garlic, salt, and pepper. Pour the dressing over the salad and gently toss. Cover and chill several hours or overnight. Serves 6.

Ensalada de Naranjas y Cebolla

Orange and Onion Salad *(picture p. 59)*

The combination of oranges with oil, vinegar, and onion
might seem unlikely, but in Valencia, where oranges grow in
countless groves and the Moors' subtle imprint still defines
the cuisine, the sweet-sour taste does not seem at all unusual.
In fact, it is captivating.

2 tablespoons golden raisins

*4 navel oranges, peeled, white
pith removed, & sliced
crosswise ¼ inch thick*

1 red onion, thinly sliced

6 tablespoons olive oil

*2 tablespoons raspberry vinegar
or red wine vinegar*

Salt & freshly ground pepper

*2 tablespoons finely chopped
blanched almonds*

12 to 18 cured black olives

*Fresh mint or parsley sprigs for
garnish*

In a small bowl, cover the raisins with hot water and let stand 10 minutes. Drain.

Arrange the oranges on a serving platter and scatter with onion.

In a small bowl, whisk together the oil, vinegar, and salt and pepper. Pour the dressing over the oranges and onion. Sprinkle the salad with almonds, raisins, and olives. Garnish with the mint sprigs. Serves 4.

Judías Estofadas con Chorizo

Bean Stew with Chorizo

If Boston baked beans are the only kind of beans with which you are familiar, these will introduce you to an entirely different taste. This is a dish that is delightfully easy to make. Spaniards love it dearly, and visitors quickly develop a taste for it, too. For the best flavor, use chorizo instead of a substitute in this dish.

1 pound dried white beans, such as great Northern

5 cups water

¼ pound chorizo sausage or other mild or breakfast sausage

¼ pound salt pork or slab bacon, cut in 1-inch cubes

1 small onion, chopped

4 garlic cloves

2 tablespoons minced parsley

1 bay leaf

Freshly ground pepper

¼ teaspoon ground cumin

1 tablespoon olive oil

1 teaspoon paprika

Salt

Cover the beans with cold water and soak overnight. Drain and rinse.

In a large soup pot, combine beans with the water, chorizo, salt pork, onion, garlic, parsley, bay leaf, pepper, and cumin. In a small cup, mix together the oil and paprika until smooth, and stir into the pot. Bring to a boil, cover, and simmer about 2 hours, or until beans are tender. Add salt to taste. Turn off the heat and let sit 20 minutes to thicken, then reheat. Serve in soup bowls, being sure to add a piece of chorizo and salt pork to each serving. Serves 4 to 6.

Huevos a la Flamenca

BAKED EGGS FLAMENCO STYLE

As vibrant in color as the costume of flamenco dancers,
these baked eggs on a bed of tomato, garnished with chorizo,
green beans, peas, pimiento, and asparagus, make a wonderful
light supper. Remove the eggs from the oven while they are
slightly underdone; they will continue cooking
in the hot casseroles.

2 tablespoons olive oil

1 garlic clove, minced

1 medium onion, finely
   chopped

1/4 pound cured ham, such as
   prosciutto, sliced 1/4 inch
   thick & diced

1/4 pound chorizo sausage or
   other mild or breakfast
   sausage, cut in 1/4-inch
   slices

1 1/2 pounds fresh or canned
   tomatoes, finely chopped

1/2 teaspoon paprika

6 tablespoons dry white wine

1 tablespoon minced parsley

Salt & freshly ground pepper

8 large eggs

8 asparagus spears, cooked

1/2 cup peas, cooked

1/4 pound green beans, cooked

1 pimiento, preferably freshly
   roasted (p. 36), cut in
   strips

Heat the oil in a skillet and sauté the garlic and onion over medium-high heat until the onion is wilted. Add the ham and chorizo and sauté 1 minute. Remove the chorizo with a slotted spoon and set aside. Mix in the tomatoes, paprika, wine, parsley, and salt and pepper. Cover, and cook ham mixture over low heat about 15 minutes.

Preheat the oven to 450°F. Divide the tomato mixture among 4 shallow individual casseroles, each about 6 inches wide. Gently slide 2 eggs into each casserole and arrange chorizo, asparagus, peas, beans, and pimiento on top. Bake until the eggs are just set, about 5 minutes in all; check for doneness after 4 minutes. Serve in the casseroles. Serves 4.

Pollo al Ajillo

Chicken in Garlic Sauce

This dish is an all-time favorite in Spain, as tasty as it is simple to make. Typically, it is cooked and served in an earthenware casserole. A very appealing first course or accompaniment would be either Sautéed Greens with Raisins and Pine Nuts (p. 37) or Manchegan Vegetable Medley (p. 34).

One 3-pound chicken, cut in small serving pieces (split the breast & cut in half again; cut each thigh in half)

Salt

5 tablespoons olive oil

6 garlic cloves, chopped, plus 1 clove, minced

1 tablespoon minced parsley

2 tablespoons dry white wine

Sprinkle chicken with salt. Heat the oil in a shallow flameproof casserole and brown the chicken over medium-high heat on all sides. Add the chopped garlic, reduce heat to medium, and cook, stirring occasionally, for 30 minutes. Stir in the minced garlic, parsley, and wine. Cover and cook for 15 minutes more, or until chicken is done and the juices run clear when the thigh is pricked with a fork. Serves 4.

Pollo al Ajillo & Acelgas con Pasas y Piñones, page 37

Pollo en Pepitoria

Chicken in Almond Sauce

This centuries-old recipe, one of the classic Spanish ways of cooking poultry, includes saffron and almonds, both of which were brought to Spain by the Moors in the eighth century. It is still served in taverns today and is as popular as it ever was.

One 3½-pound chicken, cut in serving pieces

Salt & freshly ground pepper

2 tablespoons olive oil

1 onion, chopped

1 garlic clove, minced, plus 2 cloves, mashed through a garlic press

2 teaspoons all-purpose flour

½ cup chicken broth

½ cup dry white wine

Pinch of nutmeg

1 bay leaf

20 blanched almonds, finely ground

Few threads saffron

2 tablespoons minced parsley

1 hard-boiled egg, finely chopped

Season the chicken with salt and pepper. Heat the oil in a shallow flameproof casserole and brown the chicken over medium-high heat on all sides. Stir in the onion and minced garlic and cook until onion is wilted. Stir in the flour, then add broth, wine, nutmeg, and bay leaf. Cover and cook over medium heat about 45 minutes, or until chicken is done and the juices run clear when the thigh is pricked with a fork.

Meanwhile, mash together the almonds, saffron, a pinch of salt, the pressed garlic, and 1 tablespoon parsley (preferably in a mortar; if not, in a small processor, or in a

bowl using a fork).

When the chicken is done, remove the bay leaf, stir in the almond mixture, and taste the sauce for salt. Sprinkle the egg and remaining parsley over the top. Serves 4.

Pollo al Chilindrón

Chicken Braised with Pimientos

Chilindrón describes any dish from the region of Aragón that is made with fresh red bell peppers or pimientos. The addition of onion and a little cured ham makes this an exceptional way to prepare chicken.

2 tablespoons olive oil

One 3- to 3½-pound chicken, cut in serving pieces

1 medium onion, chopped

1 garlic clove, minced

2 ounces cured ham, such as prosciutto, chopped

3 pimientos, preferably freshly roasted (p. 36), cut in strips

2 fresh or canned plum tomatoes, chopped

Salt & freshly ground pepper

Heat the oil in a shallow flameproof casserole and brown the chicken over medium-high heat on all sides. Stir in onion and garlic and cook until onion is wilted. Add ham, pimientos, tomatoes, and salt and pepper. Cover and cook over medium heat about 45 minutes, or until chicken is done and the juices run clear when the thigh is pricked with a fork. Serves 4.

Pato a la Andaluza

Duck with Olives and Sherry

Most of Spain's olive oil is produced in Andalucía, where olive trees cover some areas of land as far as the eye can see. Here, olives and the dry sherry of the region become ingredients in this famous preparation for duck.

½ cup sliced or chopped large Spanish green olives

One 4½- to 5-pound duck, as much fat removed as possible

Salt & freshly ground pepper

1 tablespoon olive oil

1 medium onion, finely chopped

2 carrots, finely chopped

3 garlic cloves, minced

¾ cup chicken broth

¼ cup dry sherry or white wine

¼ teaspoon dried thyme

1 tablespoon minced parsley

Put the olives in a small bowl, cover with warm water, and set aside.

Preheat the oven to 350°F. Sprinkle the duck inside and out with salt and pepper. Truss the duck, place it in a roasting pan, and prick it all over with a fork. Roast for 1 hour.

Meanwhile, heat the oil in a shallow flameproof casserole and sauté the onion, carrots, and garlic over medium-high heat until onion is wilted.

Cut the duck into serving pieces, removing the backbone and rib cage and discarding them. Transfer the pieces to the casserole. Pour off the fat in the roasting pan and deglaze the pan with the broth,

Pato a la Andaluza & Ensalada de Naranjas y Cebolla, page 48

scraping up any particles stuck to the bottom. Strain the liquid into the casserole.

Drain the olives. Add them to the casserole with the sherry, thyme, parsley, and salt and pepper. Bring to a boil on top of the stove, cover, then cook in the oven 1 hour. Serves 4.

Besugo a la Madrileña

Porgy Baked with White Wine

Although Madrid is in the very heart of Spain, seafood has long been its culinary passion. Even at the turn of the century fish was rushed from the Spanish coasts for the pleasure of Madrileños. *Besugo a la Madrileña* is Madrid's traditional Christmas Eve dish. Although sometimes prepared with tomato sauce, the classic version has white wine, seasonings, and a crumb topping.

½ medium onion, thinly sliced

1 medium tomato, sliced
   ¼ inch thick

2 whole garlic cloves plus 2
   cloves, minced

1 cup dry white wine

¼ cup lemon juice

½ cup olive oil

4 tablespoons minced parsley

1 bay leaf

One 4-pound porgy, red
   snapper, or other white
   fish, cleaned, with head
   left on

Salt & freshly ground pepper

6 thin lemon wedges

3 tablespoons bread crumbs

Grease a 13-by-9-inch roasting pan, and scatter the onion, tomato, and whole garlic over the bottom. Add the wine, lemon juice, oil, 2 tablespoons parsley, and bay leaf.

Preheat the oven to 350°F. Sprinkle the porgy with salt and pepper and arrange over onion and tomatoes. Make 6 incisions in the flesh and slip in the lemon wedges, leaving only the rind exposed. Bake about

1 hour, or until fish flakes easily when tested with a fork, basting occasionally with pan juices.

Meanwhile, mix together remaining parsley, minced garlic, and bread crumbs.

When only 15 minutes baking time remains, remove the bay leaf, sprinkle crumb mixture over fish, and return to the oven. Serves 4.

Merluza a la Vasca

Hake in Green Sauce

Spanish green sauces, which come from the Basque country, are so called because they are made with an abundance of parsley. Other traditional ingredients include white wine and garlic and the dish is also likely to feature peas, asparagus, clams, and hard-boiled eggs. Hake, or *merluza*, is a delicately flavored fish that makes an excellent partner for this sauce. If storing extra fish stock, let cool and refrigerate or freeze.

Fish Stock:

5 cups water

One ¾-pound small fish, such as whiting, cleaned, or 1 dozen mussels, scrubbed & debearded

1 onion

1 celery stalk

1 large carrot, cut in 1-inch pieces

1 small leek, well washed

Salt

1 bay leaf

2 parsley sprigs

4 hake or fresh cod steaks, about 1 inch thick

Salt

1½ tablespoons flour plus additional for dusting

4 tablespoons olive oil

6 garlic cloves, minced

5 tablespoons minced parsley

½ cup dry white wine

½ cup Fish Stock

¼ cup lemon juice

¼ cup fresh or frozen peas

2 hard-boiled eggs, quartered, for garnish

8 asparagus spears for garnish

8 very small clams, if desired, thoroughly scrubbed

To make the Fish Stock, in a deep pot, bring all its ingredients to a boil, cover, and simmer 1 hour. Strain.

Sprinkle the hake with salt, then dust lightly with flour. Heat 2 tablespoons oil in a large skillet and sauté fish over high heat, about 1 minute per side. Divide fish among 4 individual casseroles. Wipe out skillet.

Preheat the oven to 400°F. Heat the remaining oil in skillet, sauté garlic over medium heat, and before it browns, add 4 tablespoons parsley. Stir in 1½ tablespoons flour, then add wine, stock, and lemon juice. Stir until thickened and smooth, about 3 minutes. Add peas and salt to taste. Pour sauce over fish. Garnish dishes with egg and asparagus and bake 10 minutes.

Meanwhile, in a covered skillet, steam clams, if using, with ½ cup water over high heat. As they open, remove them and add to casseroles. Sprinkle with the remaining tablespoon of parsley. Serves 4.

Pescado a la Sal

Fish Baked in Salt

Although this fish cooks beneath a mound of coarse salt, the flesh emerges succulent and not at all salty. The secret lies in leaving the scales on the fish, then discarding both skin and scales after it has cooked. Served in fillets, the fish is accompanied by both a mayonnaise and a parsley dressing. Bake the fish in a roasting pan or other ovenproof dish attractive enough to be brought to the table.

One 4-pound porgy, sea bass, or other white fish, cleaned, head & scales left on

About 5 cups coarse salt

Mayonnaise Dressing:

½ cup mayonnaise

4 anchovy fillets, finely chopped

1 tablespoon minced parsley

¼ teaspoon dried thyme

1 teaspoon minced capers

1 garlic clove, mashed through a garlic press

Parsley Dressing:

6 tablespoons minced parsley

5 tablespoons extra-virgin olive oil

3 garlic cloves, mashed through a garlic press

Salt & freshly ground pepper

1 teaspoon lemon juice

Preheat the oven to 350°F. Arrange the fish in a greased baking dish and cover it completely with the salt. Bake for about 1½ hours, or until fish flakes easily when tested with a fork.

Meanwhile, make the Mayonnaise

Dressing by mixing all its ingredients together; make the Parsley Dressing by mixing all its ingredients together; transfer each to a small serving bowl.

To serve, scrape off as much of the salt as possible from the fish. Remove the skin and scales, then fillet the fish. Serve the fillets warm with the sauces. Serves 4.

Vieiras a la Gallega

Scallops Baked with Cured Ham

Only in Galicia in northwestern Spain will you find
freshly caught scallops served in their shells. There they are
simply prepared ~ with a sprinkling of cured ham,
onions, and bread crumbs.

2 tablespoons olive oil

*1 pound bay scallops, or sea
scallops cut in halves*

Salt & freshly ground pepper

½ cup minced onion

1 garlic clove, minced

*¼ cup minced cured ham, such
as prosciutto*

3 tablespoons dry white wine

½ cup bread crumbs

1 tablespoon minced parsley

1 teaspoon lemon juice

Grease 4 scallop shells or 4 small casseroles. Heat 1 tablespoon oil in a large skillet and sauté the scallops over high heat for 1 minute. Divide the scallops among the shells and sprinkle with salt and pepper.

Add the onion and garlic and a little more oil, if necessary, to the skillet. Cover and cook over low heat 15 minutes. Add the ham and sauté 1 minute. Stir in the wine and let it cook off. Spoon mixture over scallops.

Preheat the oven to 450°F. In a small bowl, combine the bread crumbs, parsley, lemon juice, and remaining oil. Sprinkle over the scallops. Place shells on baking sheet and bake 10 minutes. If necessary, run under the broiler to brown the top crumbs. Serve at once. Serves 4.

Zarzuela de Mariscos

Shellfish Stew

A *zarzuela*, musically speaking, is Spain's version of
light opera. Perhaps because *zarzuela* is a mix of artistic
genres ~ theater, dance, and song ~ by extension the word
applies to this dish, which combines several kinds of shellfish
with fish in a colorful sauce.

One 1½-pound live lobster or
    2 frozen lobster tails

6 tablespoons olive oil

1 pound large shrimp, shelled

1 pound fresh cod, monkfish,
    or other firm-fleshed fish
    steak

½ pound whole small squid,
    cleaned

1 small onion, chopped

1 red bell pepper, chopped

3 garlic cloves, minced

3 medium tomatoes, peeled,
    seeded, & chopped

¼ teaspoon thread saffron

2 tablespoons minced parsley

1 bay leaf

½ teaspoon dried thyme

¼ teaspoon crushed red pepper

¾ cup dry white wine

¼ cup lemon juice

Salt & freshly ground pepper

12 very small clams,
    thoroughly scrubbed

12 mussels, scrubbed &
    debearded

As close as possible to the time you are going to cook the lobster, have the fishmonger cut the claws and tail from it and break them into serving-size pieces. If using frozen lobster, cut the tails into serving-size pieces.

Fishermen in Marbella, Costa del Sol

Heat the oil in a large, shallow flame-proof casserole and quickly sauté the lobster over high heat for 3 minutes. Remove to a platter and set aside. Sauté the shrimp and fish over high heat for 1 minute and remove to platter. Add the squid to the casserole and sauté 1 minute. Add the onion, pepper, and garlic and sauté over medium heat until onion is wilted. Stir in the tomatoes, saffron, 1 tablespoon parsley, bay leaf, thyme, and crushed pepper and sauté 2 minutes. Stir in wine, lemon juice, and salt and pepper and cook, uncovered, for 10 minutes. Add the reserved seafood, cover, and simmer 10 minutes more.

In a covered skillet, steam the clams and mussels with ½ cup water over high heat. As they open, remove them and add to casserole. Cut the fish into pieces. Serve the stew in the casserole. Serves 6.

Paella a la Valenciana

Chicken and Seafood Rice

In the eyes of the world, *paella* is the quintessential Spanish dish, although it is in fact a regional specialty from Spain's eastern coast, where rice is grown. *Paella* is as spectacular in appearance as it is sensational in taste, and it makes an ideal party dish because the entire meal is cooked in one pan and much of the preparation can be done in advance.

For an authentic *paella*, you should have a large shallow metal *paella* pan and seek out a good short-grain rice, such as Valencia rice, Arborio, or California pearl rice. The rice, after all, is the most important part of the *paella* and is the key to success; all the other ingredients admit variation. For example, you could use only chicken or all seafood, or eliminate both and make a vegetable *paella*, adding lima and green beans, artichokes, carrots, and chick peas.

One 1½-pound live lobster or 2 frozen lobster tails

1½ dozen small mussels, scrubbed & debearded

1 tablespoon cornmeal or flour

5 cups chicken broth

1 bay leaf

1 small onion

½ pound small or medium shrimp in their shells

¼ teaspoon thread saffron

½ cup dry white wine

One 2½-pound chicken, hacked through bone into 1½- to 2-inch pieces

Salt

6 tablespoons olive oil

¼ pound chorizo sausage, or other mild or breakfast sausage, cut in ¼-inch slices

½ pound squid, cleaned & cut in ½-inch rings

½ cup finely chopped green bell
  pepper

½ cup finely chopped red bell
  pepper

5 garlic cloves, minced

4 medium scallions, chopped

1 teaspoon sweet paprika

2 medium tomatoes, peeled,
  seeded, & chopped

1 tablespoon minced parsley

2½ cups short-grain rice, such
  as Valencia or Arborio

½ cup fresh or frozen peas

1 pimiento, preferably freshly
  roasted (p. 36), cut in strips

As close as possible to the time you are going to cook the lobster, have the fishmonger cut the claws and tail from it and break them into serving-size pieces. If using frozen lobster, cut the tails into serving-size pieces.

Put the mussels in a bowl, cover them with salted cold water, and sprinkle with cornmeal. Refrigerate, uncovered, several hours or overnight to rid the mussels of sand. Drain and rinse mussels.

In a soup pot, combine broth with bay leaf and onion. Shell shrimp and add shells to pot with the lobster heads and small legs. Bring to a boil, cover, and simmer 40 minutes. Strain and return 4½ cups liquid to the pot. Stir in the saffron and wine. Cover and bring to a simmer.

Have all ingredients chopped and measured before beginning. Sprinkle chicken with salt. Heat oil in a large *paella* pan, placing it over 2 burners if necessary. Add the chicken, stir-fry over high heat about 10 minutes or until golden, and remove to a platter. Add the lobster pieces to pan and sauté about 3 minutes. Stir in the shrimp and chorizo, sauté 1 minute, and remove all ingredients to platter. Add squid to pan and sauté 1 minute. Stir in the peppers and sauté 3 minutes. Add garlic, scallions, paprika, tomatoes, and parsley and cook 2 minutes. (The *paella* can be made up to 2 hours in advance up to this point. Reheat in *paella* pan before proceeding.)

Preheat the oven to 375°F. Stir rice into *paella* pan. Pour in 5 cups hot broth mixture. Add peas and boil over medium-high heat, uncovered, 5 to 10 minutes, or until no longer soupy, but with enough liquid to cook the rice. Taste for salt. Stir in chorizo and shrimp. Arrange lobster, chicken, and mussels over rice, wider edge of mussels facing upward. Garnish with pimiento.

Bake *paella,* uncovered, 10 minutes. Remove from oven (the rice will be slightly undercooked), and cover loosely with foil. Let sit 5 to 10 minutes before serving. Serves 6.

Cocido Madrileño

Boiled Beef and Vegetables, Madrid Style

Cocido is Spain's meal-in-a-pot and is found in some form in every region of the country. But the *cocido* of Madrid is the most celebrated ~ a dish both peasant and grand. It is typically served in three courses: first the broth, to which noodles are often added, then the vegetables, highlighted by the chick peas, and finally the meats, although quite often the last two courses are served together. If you prepare the meats the day before and refrigerate them, you can easily remove the solidified fat that rises to the surface of the pot.

¾ pound dried chick peas

12 cups water

1 pound beef chuck

1 pound large chicken thighs

¼ pound salt pork or slab bacon

¼ pound cured ham, such as prosciutto, in a thick slice

1 beef bone

Salt & freshly ground pepper

¼ pound chorizo sausage or other mild or breakfast sausage

1 large carrot

2 large whole garlic cloves plus 1 clove, minced

1 turnip, halved

1 large leek, well washed

1 small whole onion plus 3 tablespoons chopped onion

2 parsley sprigs

Few threads saffron

6 small red potatoes, skin on

2 tablespoons olive oil

1 small green cabbage, coarsely chopped

3 ounces very thin noodles, such as fideos

Cover the chick peas with cold water and soak overnight.

In a large soup pot, combine the water, beef, chicken, salt pork, ham, beef bone, and salt and pepper. Bring to a boil, cover, and simmer 1½ hours. Let cool and refrigerate overnight if you wish to remove the fat that solidifies.

Drain and rinse chick peas. Add to soup pot (preferably in a string bag to keep them together) with the chorizo, carrot, whole garlic, turnip, leek, whole onion, parsley, and saffron. Bring to a boil, cover, and simmer about 2 hours, or until chick peas are almost tender. Add potatoes and cook 30 minutes more. Taste for salt.

Meanwhile, prepare the cabbage. Heat the oil in a large skillet and sauté minced garlic and chopped onion over medium-high heat until onion is wilted. Add cabbage, season with salt and pepper, and stir-fry 5 minutes. Cover, lower the heat, and cook 5 minutes more. Cook the noodles in a separate pan of boiling salted water until just done; drain.

To serve, strain the broth, returning enough of it to the pot to keep the remaining ingredients moist. Combine broth with noodles and serve as a first course.

Cut meats and vegetables into serving pieces. Arrange with cabbage on 1 or 2 large platters with the chick peas heaped in the center. Serves 6.

Chuletas Aliñadas con Alioli

Lamb Chops with Garlic Mayonnaise
(picture p. 41)

These chops are marinated, then grilled or broiled and
accompanied by a garlicky mayonnaise. They are particularly
good served with Poor Man's Potatoes (p. 40).

6 tablespoons olive oil

2 garlic cloves, minced

2 tablespoons minced parsley

1 tablespoon chopped fresh
thyme or ½ teaspoon dried

1½ tablespoons lemon juice

12 rib lamb chops, each ½ to
¾ inch thick

Salt & freshly ground pepper

Quick Alioli:

¾ cup mayonnaise

1 tablespoon extra-virgin olive
oil

4 garlic cloves, or to taste,
mashed through a garlic
press

1 tablespoon lemon juice

In a shallow bowl, mix together the oil, minced garlic, parsley, thyme, and lemon juice. Add the chops and coat well. Cover and refrigerate for at least 2 hours.

To make the Quick Alioli, in a small bowl, whisk together all the ingredients. Transfer to a serving bowl.

Drain chops, reserving marinade. Cook the chops under a preheated broiler or over a hot charcoal fire until browned and done to taste, basting occasionally with the marinade. Season with salt and pepper. Serve with the *alioli*. Serves 4.

Rabo de Toro

Oxtail Stew

It is only natural that this recipe ~ literally, bull's tail stew ~ hails from the bull-breeding lands of Andalucía, where bulls are as much a part of the landscape and of local festivals as they are integral to the regional cuisine. This dish gains in flavor when prepared the day before and refrigerated. With chilling, too, the fat that rises to the surface can more easily be removed.

3 to 4 pounds oxtail, cut in large pieces, trimmed of fat

Salt & freshly ground pepper

Flour for dusting

2 tablespoons olive oil

4 carrots, chopped

2 medium onions, chopped

2 garlic cloves, minced

1 teaspoon sweet paprika

½ teaspoon dried thyme

¼ teaspoon dried oregano

1½ cups dry white wine

1½ cups chicken broth

1 leek, well washed

1 tablespoon minced parsley

Sprinkle the oxtail with salt and pepper and dust with flour. Heat the oil in a large, shallow flameproof casserole, and brown the oxtail over high heat on all sides. Add the carrots, onions, and garlic and sauté over medium-high heat until the onion is wilted. Stir in the paprika, thyme, and oregano, pour in the wine and broth, and add the leek. Bring to a boil, cover, and simmer 4 hours. Adjust the seasoning, discard the leek, and sprinkle with the parsley. Serves 4 to 6.

Chuletón en Salsa de Cabrales

Steak with Blue Cheese Sauce

Cattle graze on the lush green pastures of northern Spain and there you find more beef and dairy products on the menu than anywhere else in the country. In the region of Asturias a pungent blue cheese, called Cabrales, is made from cow's milk and ripened in the mountain caves. The local beef and this cheese complement one another to create an elegant dish. Cabrales is available in the United States in well-stocked cheese shops or Spanish specialty markets.

¼ pound blue cheese, such as Cabrales or Gorgonzola, at room temperature

3 tablespoons unsalted butter

2 tablespoons heavy cream

4 tablespoons dry white wine

1 tablespoon minced parsley

1 garlic clove, minced

4 steaks of your choice, each about 1 inch thick

Salt & freshly ground pepper

In a small saucepan, mash together the cheese and 2 tablespoons butter. Whisk in the cream, 2 tablespoons wine, parsley, and garlic. Simmer, stirring frequently, until thickened and smooth, about 5 minutes. Set aside.

Sprinkle the steaks with salt and pepper. Melt the remaining butter in a large skillet.

Sauté the steaks over high heat until done to taste, and transfer to a warm serving platter. Deglaze skillet with remaining wine and stir into cheese sauce. Reheat sauce over high heat, boiling it down if necessary until thickened to a sauce consistency. Pour the sauce over the steaks and serve immediately. Serves 4.

Melocotones al Vino Tinto

Peaches Poached in Red Wine

You will find this fruit dessert all over Aragón. It is usually homemade when peaches are in season, then preserved in large jars filled with the cooking syrup. This same recipe can be used to poach pears.

6 firm but ripe peaches or
  nectarines, peeled

Lemon juice

2 cups dry red wine

1 cup water

2 cinnamon sticks, broken into
  thirds, plus additional for
  garnish

½ cup sugar

6 lemon slices

Rub peaches all over with lemon juice. In a large pot, bring the wine, water, cinnamon sticks, sugar, and 3 of the lemon slices to a boil, and simmer 15 minutes. Add peaches and simmer 20 minutes, turning them occasionally to color evenly with wine syrup. Let peaches steep in syrup several hours or overnight at room temperature.

Remove peaches from syrup and set aside. Boil the syrup down over high heat to 1 cup. Let cool completely.

Serve peaches whole or sliced in wedges. Spoon syrup over them and garnish each portion with a piece of cinnamon stick and half a lemon slice. Serves 6.

Crema Catalana

Custard with Crackly Sugar Topping

Crema Catalana is Catalunya's typical custard dessert, usually
served in earthenware dishes. The custard is soft, but the
caramelized topping is like candy brittle.

3 cups milk

1 cinnamon stick

Peel of ½ lemon

⅛ teaspoon grated nutmeg

6 egg yolks

11 tablespoons sugar

2 tablespoons cornstarch

In a heavy saucepan, bring the milk, cinnamon stick, lemon peel, and nutmeg to a boil. Reduce to a simmer and cook 5 minutes. Remove from heat and let sit 15 minutes. Discard the solids.

In a bowl, whisk the egg yolks, 5 tablespoons sugar, and cornstarch until pale yellow in color. Beat in ½ cup of the flavored milk. Pour the egg mixture into the remaining flavored milk. Cook over low heat for 10 minutes, or until custard has thickened and reached boiling point.

Remove from heat, stir, and let cool slightly. Pour into 6 wide, shallow dessert bowls. Let cool completely and refrigerate.

To make the sugar topping, just before serving sprinkle each custard with 1 tablespoon sugar. Heat a metal spatula or large metal spoon over a high flame until red hot. (Hold the handle with a pot holder.) Rest the hot metal on the sugar until it caramelizes. Rinse and dry the metal instrument and repeat with remaining custards. Serves 6.

Flan al Caramelo

Caramel Custard

Flan, baked custard with caramelized sugar sauce, has become a part of our international culinary repertoire. Indeed, the word needs no translation. *Flan* is a staple in just about every restaurant in Spain. Should you prefer an orange variation, add 1 more egg, substitute 1½ cups orange juice for the milk, and 1 teaspoon grated orange rind for the lemon zest.

½ cup plus 6 tablespoons sugar

2 tablespoons water

3 whole eggs

2 egg yolks

2½ cups milk

⅛ teaspoon salt

¼ teaspoon grated lemon zest

Whipped cream, if desired

To caramelize sugar, in a small heavy saucepan, cook ½ cup sugar and water over medium heat, stirring constantly, until the syrup turns golden in color (the sugar will crystallize before it liquefies). Immediately pour the syrup into 6 individual custard cups.

Preheat the oven to 350°F. Whisk the whole eggs and egg yolks in a large bowl until uniform in color. Whisk in the milk, remaining sugar, salt, and lemon zest. Divide the mixture among the prepared cups. Place cups in a baking pan and add enough hot water to come halfway up their sides. Bake about 45 minutes, or until a knife inserted in the custard comes out clean. Remove cups from pan and let cool. Cover and refrigerate until chilled.

Orange trees in Valencia in the Levant region

Run a knife around the edge of each cup and unmold the *flan*, spooning the caramelized sugar over it. Serve with the whipped cream, if desired. Serves 6.

Buñuelos de Viento

Light-as-the-Wind Fritters

These airy fritters, traditionally available in pastry shops on holidays and during regional festivals, are served with a dusting of powdered sugar and should be eaten right away or within a few hours of preparation. If you like, you can serve them with a syrup: In a saucepan, combine ½ cup water, ½ cup honey, 1 cup sugar, and 1 tablespoon lemon juice. Simmer over low heat for 15 minutes. Spoon the syrup over the fritters, then sprinkle them with cinnamon.

½ cup water

½ cup milk

5 tablespoons pure olive oil plus additional oil for deep-frying

¼ teaspoon salt

¼ teaspoon grated lemon zest

1 cup all-purpose flour

4 large eggs

Confectioners' sugar for dusting

In a saucepan, bring the water, milk, 5 tablespoons oil, salt, and lemon zest to a boil. Add the flour all at once, lower the heat, and stir vigorously with a wooden spoon until dough leaves the sides of the pan and forms a smooth ball. Cook, turning the dough frequently for 2 to 3 minutes. Remove from heat and cool slightly.

In a food processor, process dough 20 seconds. Add eggs and process 30 seconds.

Heat about 1 inch oil in a large skillet or electric fryer to 370°F. Drop dough by teaspoons into hot oil. The dough should puff, forming fritters and becoming golden and hollow inside. Using a slotted spoon, remove fritters to paper towels to drain and cool. Dust with sugar. Serves 8 to 10.

Polvorones

Anise-Flavored Shortbread Cookies

Polvorones ~ from the Spanish word *polvo*, or "dust" ~ are so named because they are extremely delicate and crumble easily. That is why they are often sold individually wrapped in tissue paper in pastry shops. Traditionally *polvorones* are made with lard, but butter also produces a wonderfully short cookie.

1 tablespoon confectioners' sugar plus about 1 cup for dusting

1 egg yolk

1 teaspoon lemon juice

2 teaspoons brandy

2 cups all-purpose flour

½ teaspoon ground anise seeds

1 teaspoon grated lemon zest

2 tablespoons cinnamon

⅛ teaspoon salt

½ pound unsalted butter, softened

In a cup, stir together 1 tablespoon sugar, egg yolk, lemon juice, and brandy until smooth. In a large bowl, combine flour with the anise, lemon zest, cinnamon, and salt.

In an electric mixer, cream the butter well. Beat in the egg yolk mixture, then beat in half of the flour mixture. Using a wooden spoon, gradually incorporate remaining flour mixture.

Preheat the oven to 300°F. Roll out the dough to about ⅜ inch thick on a floured surface. Using a 3-inch fluted-edge round cookie cutter, cut out cookies. Bake on an ungreased baking sheet about 30 minutes, or until the cookies are lightly browned and firm to the touch. Let cool about 2

minutes. Sift sugar onto a sheet of waxed paper. Dredge cookies in sugar. Arrange cookies on a serving plate and dust with remaining sugar. Makes 10 to 12 cookies.

Leche Frita

Fried Milk

Although its literal translation is "fried milk," *leche frita* is custard that is firm enough to cut. Sliced into squares, it is then dipped in egg and flour and fried, becoming crunchy on the outside and creamy within. The squares are best eaten right away, but can be kept warm for a brief time in a low oven.

2 cups milk

1 cinnamon stick

Peel of 1 lemon

3 egg yolks

¼ cup all-purpose flour

3 tablespoons cornstarch

¾ cup sugar

1 teaspoon vanilla

½ teaspoon cinnamon

2 large whole eggs, lightly beaten

1 teaspoon water

Pure olive oil for deep-frying

Flour for dusting

In a large saucepan, bring the milk, cinnamon stick, and lemon peel to a boil, and simmer 15 minutes. Discard solids.

In another saucepan, whisk the egg yolks. Stir in flour, cornstarch, and ¼ cup sugar. Very gradually whisk in the hot milk and cook over medium heat, stirring constantly, until a very thick and smooth custard forms and no cornstarch taste remains. (Whisk briefly, if necessary, to eliminate any lumps.) Remove from heat, stir in vanilla, and cool 5 minutes, stirring occasionally to release steam. Pour custard into a greased 8-inch-square cake pan and

A shepherd with his flock on Ibiza, one of the Balearic Islands

let cool completely; then chill, lightly covered with waxed paper, until custard has solidified.

In a small bowl, combine the remaining ½ cup sugar and cinnamon; set aside. In a shallow bowl, beat eggs lightly with water. Cut the custard into 2-inch squares. Heat about ½ inch oil to 370°F. in a skillet. Dredge custard squares carefully in flour, dip in the beaten egg, and fry in the oil until golden, turning once. Remove the squares with a slotted spoon to paper towels to drain and cool. Dust with cinnamon and sugar mixture. Serves about 6 to 8.

Pestiños

Honey-Coated Fried Pastries

Flavored with anise and lemon, bathed in honey, and dusted
with powdered sugar, *pestiños*, typical of La Mancha, are
irresistible. These pastries are best when prepared
a day in advance.

½ cup pure olive oil plus
   additional oil for deep-
   frying

Peel of ½ lemon

1 tablespoon anise seeds

2 cups all-purpose flour

⅛ teaspoon salt

½ cup dry white wine

Honey for drizzling

Confectioners' sugar for dusting

Cinnamon for dusting

In a small skillet, heat the ½ cup oil, lemon peel, and anise seeds over low heat and remove from heat when seeds begin to brown. Let sit 10 minutes. Strain, discard solids, and reserve the oil.

In a large bowl, combine flour and salt. Add wine and reserved oil and work into a ball, adding a little more flour if dough is too sticky. Cover and let sit for 1 hour.

Roll out the dough on a floured surface into a rectangle about ⅛ inch thick. Using a sharp knife, cut into rectangular strips about 1¼ inches wide and 2 inches long.

Heat about 1 inch oil to 370°F. in a large skillet or electric fryer. Add as many dough strips as will fit comfortably and deep-fry, turning once, until golden and puffed. With a slotted spoon, remove pastries to paper towels to drain and cool. Drizzle with honey, slightly thinned with a little water, and dust with confectioners' sugar and cinnamon. Makes about 60 pastries.

Manzanas Asadas Rellenas de Almendra

Almond-Filled Baked Apples

These apples are filled with some of the most appealing flavors of Spain: sherry, almonds, raisins, and cinnamon. You may top them with whipped cream or serve with ice cream.

3 tablespoons cream sherry

2 tablespoons golden raisins

4 large baking apples, such as McIntosh, Granny Smith, or Rome Beauties

Lemon juice

¾ cup water

5 tablespoons sugar

2 ounces almonds, ground

¼ teaspoon grated lemon zest

¼ teaspoon cinnamon

⅛ teaspoon grated nutmeg

3 tablespoons butter, melted & cooled

In a small saucepan, combine the sherry and raisins. Bring to a boil, remove from heat, and set aside for 10 minutes. Peel the apples and rub them with lemon juice. Core the apples from the top, leaving a ½ inch at the bottom of each apple.

Strain sherry into a shallow baking dish. Stir in the water and 1 tablespoon sugar.

Preheat the oven to 350°F. In a small bowl, combine the raisins, almonds, remaining sugar, lemon zest, cinnamon, nutmeg, and butter. Fill apples with the almond mixture and arrange in baking dish. Bake 30 minutes, basting apples occasionally. Cover lightly with foil and bake 15 to 30 minutes more, or until apples are tender. Spoon juices over apples and serve warm or at room temperature. Serves 4.

WEIGHTS

OUNCES AND POUNDS	METRICS
¼ ounce	7 grams
⅓ ounce	10 grams
½ ounce	14 grams
1 ounce	28 grams
1¾ ounces	50 grams
2 ounces	57 grams
2⅔ ounces	75 grams
3 ounces	85 grams
3½ ounces	100 grams
4 ounces (¼ pound)	114 grams
6 ounces	170 grams
8 ounces (½ pound)	227 grams
9 ounces	250 grams
16 ounces (1 pound)	464 grams
1.1 pounds	500 grams
2.2 pounds	1,000 grams (1 kilogram)

TEMPERATURES

°F (FAHRENHEIT)	°C (CENTIGRADE OR CELSIUS)
32 (water freezes)	0
108-110 (warm)	42-43
140	60
203 (water simmers)	95
212 (water boils)	100
225 (very slow oven)	107.2
245	120
266	130
300 (slow oven)	149
350 (moderate oven)	177
375	191
400 (hot oven)	205
425	218
450	232
500 (very hot oven)	260

LIQUID MEASURES

tsp.: teaspoon
Tbs.: tablespoon

SPOONS AND CUPS	METRIC EQUIVALENTS
1 tsp.	5 milliliters (5 grams)
2 tsp.	10 milliliters (10 grams)
3 tsp. (1 Tbs.)	15 milliliters (15 grams)
3⅓ Tbs.	½ deciliter (50 milliliters)
¼ cup	59 milliliters
⅓ cup	1 deciliter less 1⅓ Tbs.

SPOONS AND CUPS	METRIC EQUIVALENTS
⅓ cup + 1 Tbs.	1 deciliter (100 milliliters)
1 cup	¼ liter less 1¼ Tbs.
1 cup + 1¼ Tbs.	¼ liter
2 cups	½ liter less 2½ Tbs.
2 cups + 2½ Tbs.	½ liter
4 cups	1 liter less 1 deciliter
4⅓ cups	1 liter (1,000 milliliters)

INDEX